伊伊，春节快乐！

Happy Chinese New Year, Elena!

Written by: Dingli Stevens, Illustrated by: Kun Liang

常青圖書 Cypress Books

Happy Chinese New Year, Elena! 伊伊，春节快乐！(Chinese-English Bilingual Edition)
Written by Dingli Stevens, Illustrated by Kun Liang
Project Management: Antong Consulting Agent

First Published in Great Britain in 2019 by Cypress Book Co. UK Ltd.
Unit 6 Provident Industrial Estate, Pump Lane, Hayes UB3 3NE, United Kingdom
Tel: 00442088480572
Email: info@cypressbooks.com

ISBN: 978-1-8457-0040-9
Printed in China

www.cypressbooks.com

这本书属于

This book belongs to

_____

春节，是农历一月一日，俗称正月初一。是中国最重要的传统节日。
春节是辞旧迎新的节庆，家家户户欢聚一堂，一起迎接新的一年。

春节快乐

Chinese New Year, also called Lunar New Year or the Spring Festival, falls on the first day of the Chinese lunar calendar.
It bids farewell to the old year, welcomes in the new year, and is the biggest festival in China.

过春节也叫过年。
年前，伊伊从伦敦飞到北京，
和爷爷奶奶一起过年。

Chinese People call the whole celebration "Guonian".
Before Chinese New Year, Elena travelled from London to Beijing to celebrate the Chinese New Year with her grandparents.

春节前两天，爸爸妈妈忙着打扫屋子，伊伊帮奶奶贴春联。

看着一旁玩舞狮的妹妹，
伊伊好奇地问："奶奶，为什么过年要舞狮子呀？"
奶奶说："图个好兆头！因为狮子有力量、很勇敢，舞狮能保佑我们在新的
一年里平平安安、顺顺利利！狮子可以一直保护你，陪着你，帮助你。"

Days before the festival, Elena helped Grandma decorate her front door with red "Spring Festival Couplets". Elena's parents cleaned the house, which symbolises removing the old to make way for the new.

Elena's little sister Gabby was playing a lion costume.
"Grandma, why do we have lion dances during the Chinese New Year?" Elena asked curiously.
"For good fortune! We believe the lion dance ushers in a peaceful and prosperous new year because lions are strong and brave. The lion will be with you, to protect and help you." Grandma answered.

正月初六的早晨，
传来一阵鞭炮锣鼓声。
"舞狮队来啦！"
小朋友们奔走相告。
大家纷纷找好位置，
等着看舞狮队表演。

On the sixth day of the New Year, Elena woke up to the sound of drums and gongs, as well as exploding firecrackers.

"The lion dance is coming!" shouted children excitedly.

Everyone was ready for the lion dance!

"咚咚锵，咚咚锵！"
狮子随着锣鼓声，上蹦下跳。

"快看啊，他跳起来啦！"
现场一阵欢呼。

Dong dongqiang, dong dongqiang!
The lion danced to the sound of drums and gongs.

"Look, he is jumping!"
The audience cheered.

人潮散去，伊伊捡起滚落在地上的彩球，还给领头的狮子。

After the crowd dispersed, Elena picked up the coloured ball rolling
along the ground, and passed it back to the leading lion.

"谢谢你！你叫什么名字？"

"Thank you! What's your name?"
the lion said.

"不客气！我叫伊伊！"

"You're welcome. I am Elena."
she answered.

伊伊指着地上的格子房，说："你可以陪我跳房子么？"

"好啊！我很愿意陪你玩。"

狮子建议："把彩球放在房顶数字8上；你回答我一个春节的问题，我就往前跳一格，你来帮我拿到彩球好不好？"

Pointing to the hopscotch court on the ground, Elena asked: "Can we play hopscotch?"
"Sure, I would love to!" the lion nodded. "Look, I'll put the coloured ball here at Number Eight and I'll hop over one square each time you answer one of my Chinese New Year questions. Help me to reach the ball, will you?" the lion suggested.

狮子问："第一问！你在学校是怎么庆祝春节的呢？"
伊伊开心地说："回答！我们学校有春节庆祝表演。
我和同学们一起穿着旗袍表演歌舞《恭喜，恭喜》。"

"First question! How did you celebrate the Spring Festival in your school?" The lion asked.
"We had a celebration in our school. I performed a song and dance routine named *Gong Xi, Gong Xi*
in my traditional qipao together with my classmates." Elena answered happily.

"我还带柑橘去学校，跟同学们交换。"伊伊接着说。
"柑橘的颜色与'金子'相近，'橘'与'吉'发音相似。
柑橘象征着大吉大利，富贵如意。"狮子点点头。

"I also brought mandarin oranges to exchange with
my classmates." Elena added.
"Great! Mandarin oranges look like gold.
They symbolise good luck and prosperity."
the lion nodded.

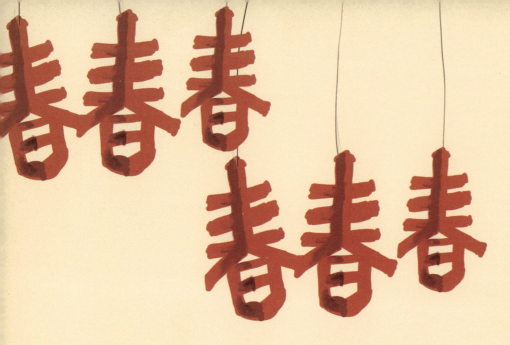

狮子又问："你在学校做什么特别的手工了么？"
伊伊马上回答："有啊！我们剪纸做'春'字。
我们还把'春'字做成了立体卡片。"

"Did you make any special handicrafts in school?"
the lion asked.
Elena answered quickly.
"Yes! We did Chinese paper cutting.
We cut lots of Chinese character '春' as decorations.
We made pop-up cards too."

"这是我们做立体卡片的办法！"

"This is how we made our pop-up cards!"

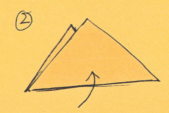

1. 准备好剪刀、胶棒、笔、一张A4的红色卡片纸、一张正方形的金色纸。

Prepare scissors, glue, a pen, an A4 piece of red card-paper and a square piece of gold paper.

2. 将金色纸沿对角线对折成三角形。

Fold the gold paper into a triangle.

3. 用笔描出半个"春"字。

Write half of the Chinese character "春" (spring) on the triangle.

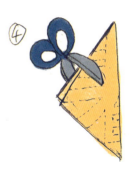 

4. 用剪刀顺着笔画剪；展开，就是一个完整的"春"字。

Now cut along the lines and unfold to get the whole character for "春".

5. 把红色的纸对折并打开，把剪好的"春"字的角上抹上胶棒，贴在红色纸的中间。

Now fold the red card-paper in half and stick your "春" in the middle.

6. 重新对折红色的纸，可以在封面上写上"新春快乐"等祝福的话。卡片就做好了。

Finally, you can write "Happy Chinese New Year" on the front cover!

狮子问："我跳到数字3啦！伊伊，农历年的最后一夜是除夕。你在除夕干什么了？"

"The third question! Chinese New Year's Eve is called Chuxi. It is the last evening of the lunar year. What did you do on Chuxi, Elena?" the lion asked.

伊伊说："吃年夜饭！然后，我们全家一起守岁。
当新年来到时，我们就开始放鞭炮。噼里啪啦，噼里啪啦！"

"We had the reunion dinner. Then I stayed up until midnight with my family.
We let off firecrackers on the arrival of the new year. Pilipala! Pilipala!"
Elena mimicked the sound of firecrackers.

"伊伊，你们年夜饭的主食是什么啊？" 狮子问。

"饺子啊！" 伊伊说。

"What special dish did you have for the reunion dinner?" the lion asked.
"Dumplings!" Elena exclaimed.

狮子又问："你知道怎么做饺子吗？"

伊伊自豪地回答："我知道，奶奶教我包饺子了！"

"Do you know how to make dumplings?"
"Yes, I do. My grandma taught me."

面皮
Dumpling skin

"饺子有各种各样的馅儿，有肉馅儿，也有素馅儿。
我最爱西红柿鸡蛋馅儿的。"伊伊说。

"There are many kinds of dumpling fillings.
My favourite filling is tomato and egg!" Elena said.

葱
Leek

鸡蛋 Egg

虾 Shrimp

饺子 Dumplings

肉 Meat

茄子
Aubergine

西红柿 Tomato

馅儿
Dumpling filling

韭菜
Chives

蔬菜
Vegetables

鱼肉
Fish

羊肉
Lamb

粉条
Glass noodles

豆腐
Tofu

World of Books
Sell Your Books

Turn your unwanted books into cash

scan to earn

Get 15% extra

with code: **SELLYOURBOOKS**

sell.worldofbooks.com

World of Books

Sell Your Books

As simple as 1, 2, 3:

1 Scan your books with our Sell Your Books app

2 Get an instant price for your book

3 Ship your books to us for free and get paid.

Reasons to trade:

Clear clutter

Earn money

Fee free

get trading now

sell.worldofbooks.com

狮子问：
"春节时候，你最喜欢吃什么呀？"

伊伊拍着手跳了起来：
"我最爱吃火锅了。
火锅里可以烫各种东西，
比如：羊肉片、豆腐、
青菜、鱼片、粉条……
妈妈说，火锅红红火火，热气腾腾，
大家新的一年会开心、日子更好！"

The lion asked:

"What is your favourite dish for Chinese New Year?"

"Hot-pot!" Elena jumped up clapping her hands,
"You can put lots of different foods into the hot-pot:
lamb, tofu, vegetables, glass noodle….and,
my mum said the hot-pot symbolizes the coming year
being happier and better too!"

"我要往数字6跳啦！
大年初一那天，
你干的第一件事儿是什么？"
狮子问。

"What was the first thing
you did on the first day of
Chinese New Year?"
the lion asked.

给爷爷奶奶拜年呀，
伊伊一边笑着说，一边拱手作揖，
"新年快乐，恭喜发财！
然后他们就给我发红包，里面有压岁钱。"

"Greet Grandma and Grandpa!"
Elena recalled cheerfully,
while bowing with both hands held in front,
"Happy New Year, Gong Xi Fa Cai!
Then they gave me a hongbao,
which is a red envelope filled with lucky money."

"伊伊，大年初二你干什么了？"狮子问。

"我们全家去逛庙会了。有很多好吃的和好看的东西，太有趣了。"伊伊一脸幸福地说。

"What did you do on the second day of Chinese New Year?" the lion asked.

"We went to the Temple Fair. There were so many yummy foods to try and so many interesting things to see!" Elena recalled blissfully.

"庙会上有各种表演，舞龙灯的、踩高跷的、划旱船的！"伊伊说，"在伦敦，中国城在春节期间就有庆祝活动，跟庙会很像。去年爸爸妈妈带我去过呢。"

"I saw puppet shows, dragon dancing, stilt-walking and other performances in the Temple Fair."
Elena said, "In London, there are similar celebrations in China Town too! My parents took me to

"伊伊，我的最后一跳啦。春节期间，
你最开心的事儿是什么？"狮子问。
"和爸爸一起去后海滑冰，坐冰板凳！"
伊伊笑着回忆。

"This will be the last square, Elena!
What's your favourite Chinese New
Year activity?" the lion asked.
"Ice-skating with my dad! It is so
much fun!" Elena smiled.

狮子成功地跳进房顶的格子，高高举起那个彩球。
Hopping onto the eighth square, the lion picked up
the coloured ball and raised it high.

"伊伊，谢谢你帮我跳到房顶！" 狮子说。
"Thank you for helping me, Elena! We made it together!"

"谢谢你陪我玩儿！ 大狮子，
以后我还可以跟你玩儿么？"
伊伊问。
"Thank you for playing with me, lion!
Can we do this again in the future?"

"当然可以啦！" 狮子开心地说。
"Of course!" the lion said happily.

"我永远愿意听你说，陪你玩。"

"I will always love playing and chatting with you."

"春节快乐，伊伊！"

"Happy Chinese New Year, Elena!"

"狮子再见！"

"See you later, lion!"

跟着伊伊过春节，跟着伊伊学中文

春节	Spring Festival	chūn jié 春 节
	Spring Festival couplets	chūn lián 春 联
	Lion dance	wǔ shī 舞 狮
	Lion	shī zi 狮 子
	Hopscotch	tiào fáng zi 跳 房 子

Paper cutting

jiǎn zhǐ
剪 纸

Chinese New Year's Eve

chú xī
除 夕

Dumplings

jiǎo zi
饺 子

Temple Fair

miào huì
庙 会

Ice-skating

huá bīng
滑 冰